This journal belongs to:

____

Numbers

7
One

3
Three

4
Four

5

five

6

six

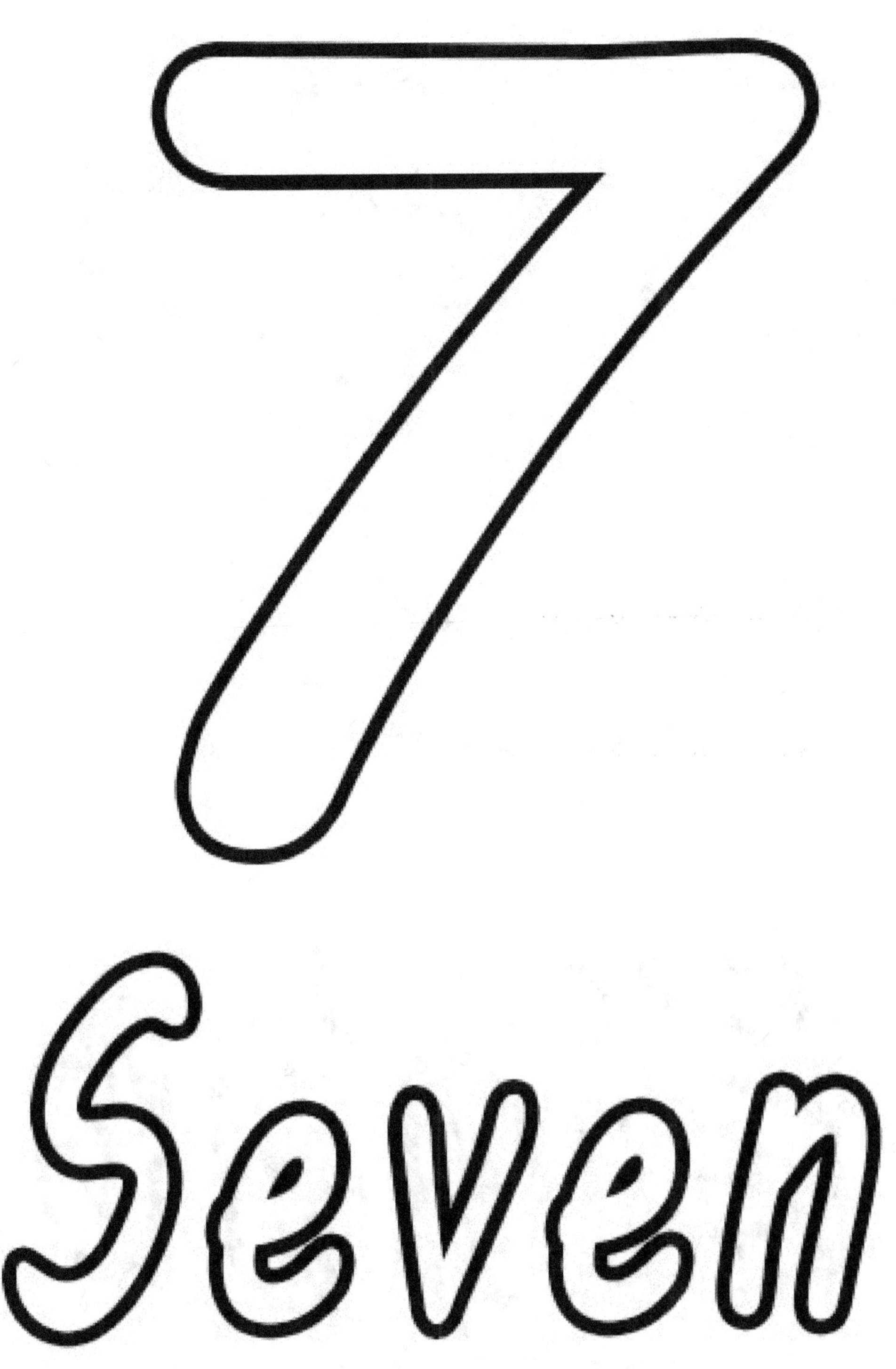

7
Seven

8
Eight

9
Nine

10

Ten

Vegetables &
Fruits

Carrot

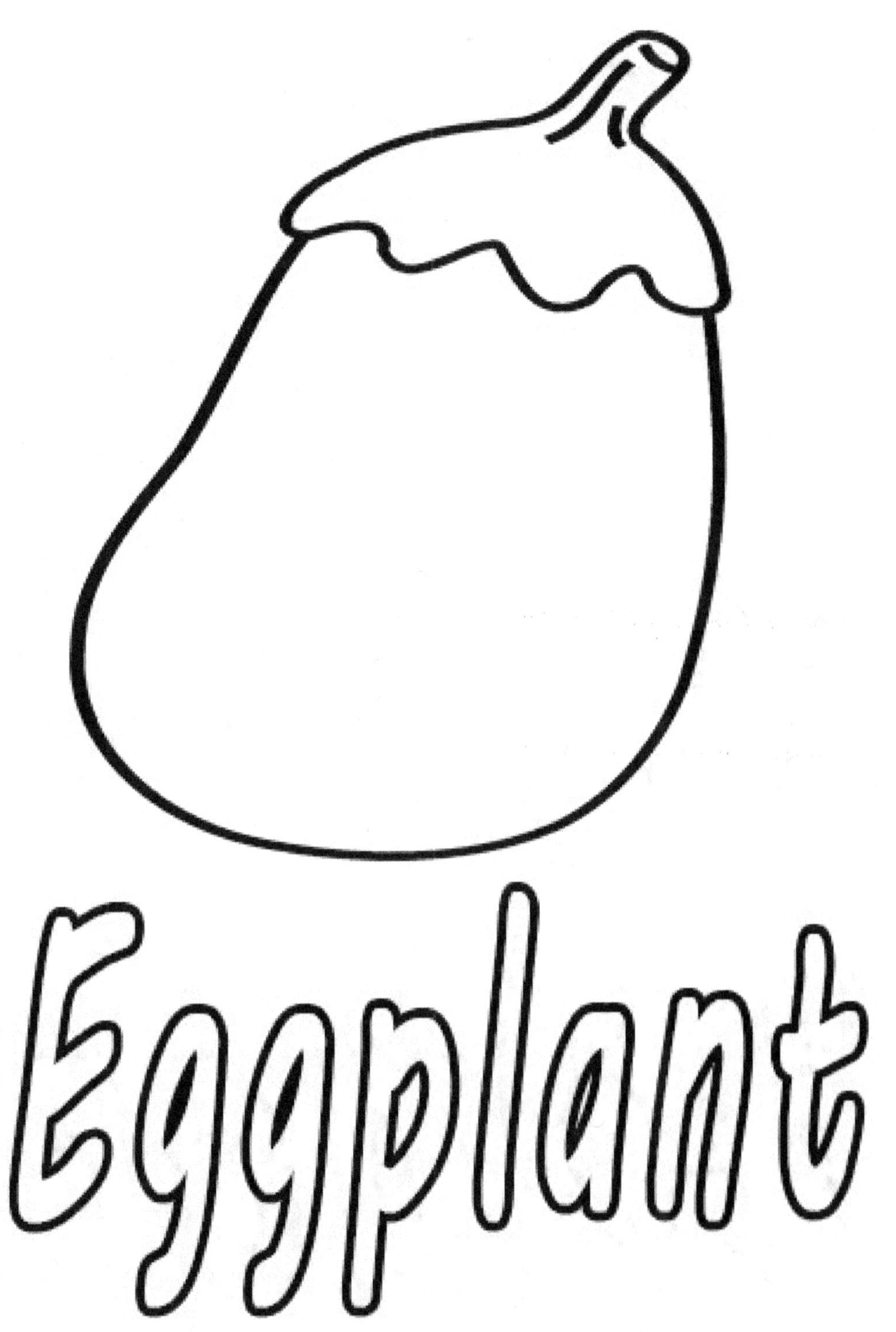
Eggplant

Lemon

Pumpkin

Tomato

Apple

Orange

Pineapple

Straw

Berry

Water

Melon

Animals Alphabet

Alligator

Aa

Bear

B b

Cow

C c

Deer
Dd

Elephant

E e

Fox

Ff

Giraffe

G g

Hedgehog

H h

Iguana

l i

Jellyfish

Jj

Kangaro

K k

Lion

L l

Monkey

Mm

Narwhal

Nn

Owl

Oo

Panda

P p

Quail

Q q

Rabbit

Rr

Snail

Ss

Tiger

Tt

Unicorn

Vulture

Vv

Whale

Ww

Xiphias

Xx

Yak

Yy

Zebra

Zz

www.ingramcontent.com/pod-product-compliance
Lightning Source LLC
Chambersburg PA
CBHW070759250726
48662CB00004B/1885